# Pocket Book

## For Students
## In Italy

**Foreword by:**
**The Ambassador of Italy in India**
Lorenzo Angeloni

**STERLING**

*To all my Indian Students*

With a hearthfelt thank-you for the wonderful journey over the last five years.

STERLING PAPERBACKS
An imprint of
Sterling Publishers (P) Ltd.
Regd. Office: A1/256 Safdarjung Enclave,
New Delhi-110029. CIN: U22110DL1964PTC211907
Email: mail@sterlingpublishers.in
www.sterlingpublishers.in
*Pocket Book For Students in Italy*
© 2019, Paola Martani
ISBN 978 93 86245 60 1
All rights are reserved.
*Printed and Published in India by*
Sterling Publishers Pvt. Ltd.,
Plot No 13, Ecotech-III, Greater Noida - 201306, U.P. India.

# Foreword

This delightful new pocket guide has been put together in order to provide practical guidance to Indian students embarking on a course of study in Italy.

I believe that this handbook will prove an invaluable source of information, neither too detailed nor too sparse and I am sure that even the most confident traveler would find it useful in their journey in Italy. A set of beautiful illustrations complements the abundant and helpful tips and definitions.

As the reader may be already aware, student mobility to Italy offers great opportunities since Italy speaks many languages: from Architecture, Arts, Design and Fashion to Research and Innovation. And, speaking of languages, this book also includes a basic vocabulary for daily interactions and a collection of basic Italian phrases for the most common situations.

I am confident that this project will help facilitate people-to-people exchanges between Italy and India and I warmly recommend this guide to those who are planning to invest on their personal growth by studying in Italy.

Lastly, I would like to commend the author Paola Martani for writing this handbook and coordinating its publication with competence and passion.

I wish you success in your endeavor and I encourage you to explore Italy's many wonders, suitably equipped with this resourceful pocket guide.

Lorenzo Angeloni
Ambassador of Italy in New Delhi

# From the author

As I approach my 7th anniversary of living in India, and my 5th year as Course Coordinator at the Italian Embassy Cultural Center in New Delhi and as a professor of Italian Culture, this project seems to be the most appropriate gift that I could give to this country.

Over these years I have seen students who, after growing passionate about the '*Italian dream*', have decided to spend parts of their lives in my native country. Some of them I have accompanied to the airport boarding gates, others I have welcomed back after years abroad to hear of the smiles and also of the problems which they encountered in Italy.

For the love I have for all Indian students, for the love I have for these two countries, for my absolute conviction that the amalgamation of our cultures can enrich not only the individual but the society, I dedicate these pages to all the Indian students. who will decide to study in the '*beautiful country*'. I pray that this pocket book will be of use for clarifying the bureaucracy you will face daily, and that it will to help you find the right words to not only survive but to thrive during your stay. It brings me joy to know that I will always be in the pocket of the hundreds of students whom I carry in my heart, and that I will indirectly help those students I never knew.

I wish you all success in your studies and in your life in (and after) Italy. I wish you this as I thank you for what you have given me during my years in India.

Paola Martani

India Gate
New Delhi, India

# Acknowledgements

It seems hard to believe that such a small pocket book required so many months of work and passion.

In reality, it required so much from many people, and I would like to thank them all for their support - which, as usual, never failed.

Special thanks must go to Chiara Petracca, Head of the Press and Cultural Affairs - Italian Embassy, the person who first had the idea for this booklet.

I also send warm thanks to the Director of the Italian Embassy Cultural Centre, Andrea Baldi, for having spent many afternoons, reading and re-reading these pages in order to be sure that the information conveyed is as correct, as clear, and as complete as possible.

Thanks to Uni-Italia, for always being available to complete the information we lacked on the various Italian universities.

Thanks to the Embassy of Italy in New Delhi, for revising all parts of the manuscript, and for handling the bureaucracy and the various documents necessary for Indian students who wish to travel to Italy.

To my team, I thank you for your help and your shared passion to see Italy and India united.

Wine Farm
Toscana, Italia

# Contents

**Studying in Italy** — 13
: Education — 14
: Scholarship and Grant Opportunities — 21

**First steps** — 25
: Renewal of Residence Permit — 29
  (Permesso di Soggiorno)
: Documents you must always carry in Italy — 32

**Practicalities of Living in Italy** — 35
: Finding accommodation — 36
: Healthcare — 42
   : The ASL — 42
   : The Tessera Sanitaria — 46
   : In Case of Emergency — 47
: Transportation — 50
   : Driving — 56
   : Bicycling — 56
: Travel and lodging — 59
: Taking Language Courses — 65
: Employment in Italy — 66
: Banking and Finance — 68
: Shopping — 71
: Emergency details — 76
: Contacts in Delhi — 79

Tea Gardens of Munnar
Kerala, India

# Contents

**Language kit** — 81
: Greetings — 82
: Polite expressions — 83
: Introduction — 84
: Numbers and Counting — 90
: Days - I giorni — 92
: Months - I Mesi — 93
: At restaurants — 95
: Useful Questions — 100

Vista dal Ponte di Rialto
Venezia, Italia

# Education

**The Italian Higher Education System – an overview**

Many of Italy's Universities are amongst the oldest in the Western world, and the country has an ancient tradition of scholarship and innovation- particularly in the fields of design, architecture, applied sciences, and the arts.

**Italy has 68 state universities and 17 private universities recognized by the Government.**

There are also 137 AFAM institutes (Higher Education in Art and Music) offering training, production, and research activities in the field of art, specifically the visual arts, music, dance, drama and design. These include:

: The National Dramatics Academy
: The National Dance Academy
: 20 State Academies of Fine Arts
: 20 Legally Recognized Academies of Fine Arts
: 55 Music Conservatories
: 18 State Recognized Private Acadamies of Music
: 5 Superior Institutes for Artistic Industry (ISIA)
: 17 Institutions Authorized to Issue Titles for Higher
  Education in Art, Music and Dance

The education offered by universities (and AFAM Institutes) is divided into 3 phases. Students may enroll after completing 13 years of pre-university education.

This table summarizes each phase:

| | Italian Qualifications | | Credits | Years |
|---|---|---|---|---|
| First Phase | Laurea | Bachelor's Degree | 180 | 3 |
| Second Phase | Laurea Magistrale | Master's Degree | 120 | 2 |
| | Master Universitario di 1° livello ^ | 1st Level Specializing Master | ≥ 60 | |
| | Laurea Magistrale ciclo unico * | Single-Cycle Master's Program | 300-360 | 5-6 |
| Third Phase | Dottorato di ricerca | PhD | | 3 |
| | Specializzazione di 2° livello | Postgraduate Diploma Course | | 2 |
| | Master universitario di 2° livello | 2nd Level Specializing Master | ≥ 60 | |

^ This qualification does not give access to a Ph.D.
* Offered in some universities and for some subjects (Medicine, Pharmacology, Law)

Duomo Nuovo
Brescia, Italia

# Education

**Statistics**

: In the previous years, the average enrolment in Italian Universities was 1,654,680, with 919,309 girls (more than 55% per cent). 76,351 students were foreigners (approximately 4.6%). Only 176,158 students were enrolled in private institutions.

: In 2016, the total number of graduated students was 311,799. 180,121 of them were girls, and 12,295 were foreigners.

: In the same period, the total enrolment in AFAM Institutes was 67,454, with 38,037 girls (more than 56%), and 11,588 foreigners (17%).

**Financial Information**

The exact cost of tuition fees depends upon several factors. For example, owing to significant government funding, public universities have much lower tuition fees than private universities. The quality of education, however, is at a comparably high level across all officially recognised institutions of higher education.

Regular fees for EU and non-EU students depend on the students' family income and on the program applied for. Fees range from a minimum of 900€ to a maximum of 4.000€ per year at a public university, and from 6.000€ to around 20.000€ per year at a private one. Tuition fees do not include the cost of student accommodation or books.

# Conversation

> **Avete questo libro?**

> Do you have this book?

> **È per l'esame del Professor Rossi?**

> Is it for Professor Rossi's exam?

> **Sì, esatto. È per l'esame di filosofia.**

> Yes, exactly. It's for the exam in philosophy.

# Vocabulary

|  |  |
|---|---|
| Libro | Book |
| Quaderno | Notebook |
| Dispensa | Professor's note |
| Penna | Pen |
| Matita | Pencil |
| Gomma | Eraser |
| Temperino | Pencil sharpener |
| Righello | Ruler |
| Astuccio | Pencil case |
| Quaderno a quadretti | Squared notebook |
| Quaderno a righe | Lined notebook |

Val di Fassa, Dolomiti
Trentino, Italia

# Scholarship and grant opportunities

There are 3 different categories of scholarships offered:
1. Scholarships/grants offered by the Italian government
    : These are usually advertised online in the spring time for studies starting the following academic year

    : Applicants must provide a certificate of proficiency in Italian language. The minimum level required is A2 within the Common European Framework of Reference for Languages (CEFR).

    : Grants are offered to pursue study, training, and/or research programs at Italian Higher Education Institutes (both public and legally recognized private institutions).

    : For Master's Degree (Laurea Magistrale 2^ ciclo), Courses of Higher Higher Education in Arts, Music and Dance (AFAM), PhD programs and research under academic supervision (progetti in co-tutela), the grants are usually awarded for a period of 6 or 9 months.

    : Grants for Italian language and culture courses are awarded exclusively to students attending an Italian course at a University for a period of 3 months.

    : For more information: www.ambnewdelhi.esteri.it | www.iicnewdelhi.esteri.it | www.esteri.it | https://studyinitaly.esteri.it/en/home_borse |

# Scholarship and grant opportunities

2. **Scholarships/grants offered to foreign students by individual universities.**

    : Many universities offer a variety of scholarships every year to talented international students.

    : More information can generally be found on their websites, and on the website of the Italian Ministry of Foreign Affairs: https://www.esteri.it/mae/en/servizi/stranieri/opportunita/borse-di-studio-offerte-dalle-universita.html

3. **Scholarships offered at the European Union level that you can use to study in Italy**

    : The Invest Your Talent in Italy program offers funding for students from 15 different countries (including India) to undertake a range of Master's and Postgraduate qualifications in Engineering, Advanced Technologies, Architecture, Design, Economics and Management.

    : These courses are taught in English at 23 prestigious Italian Universities

    : The aim is to improve academic, technical and professional skills, and the courses include on-the-job training at leading Italian companies

: A three or four-year Bachelor's degree is required as general entry qualification, but specific entry requirements will vary between courses.

: The scholarship will cover a 9 month period of study, generally starting in October. Applications are generally open from November and must be submitted by January in the year one wants to be enrolled.*

: The scholarship is worth 8,100 euro per year and, in case of attendance of a two year course, it can be renewed for the second academic year.

: For more information: https://eeas.europa.eu/delegations/india/672/study-eu_en). www.postgradinitaly.esteri.it

**\* Please check the link given above for the exact information.**

Fontana di Trevi
Roma, Italia

# On arrival

**If you arrive at Rome's airport,** it will take 30 minutes by train to reach the city centre. Take the direct train to Termini station (central station), or the local train FL1, which makes several stops. You can also choose to take the bus to Termini station, which takes 1 hour, or you could take a taxi.

**If you arrive at Milan's airport,** you can take the train from the T1 to the city's central station. You could also take a bus or taxi. To go to Turin, you can take the train from T1 to Torino Porta Nuova station.

1. **As soon as you arrive in the country** you will need to ensure that you have an entry visa (Visto di ingresso) linked to your valid passport (Passaporto)

2. **If you want to study in Italy** then simply having an entry visa is not enough- you will need to have a Permit to Stay (Permesso di Soggiorno) in the country.

    : You will need to apply for Permesso di Soggiorno within **8 business days** of your arrival

    : You can do this at your local Prefecture office (Prefettura UTG), where you will find the Unified Desk for Immigration (Sportello Unico per l'immigrazione)

    : After this initial step, you will be able to go online to complete the remainder of the application

# Conversation

|  |  |
|---|---|
| Da quale gate parte il volo? | From which gate does the flight leave? |
| Dove posso cambiare dei soldi? | Where can I exchange money? |
| Dov'è la fermata del taxi? | Where is the taxi stand? |
| Dov'è la fermata degli autobus? | Where is the bus stop? |
| Dov'è la fermata dei treni? | Where is the stop for the train? |

Quick Tip: It is better to address an officer with *'Salve'* (polite), instead of *'Ciao'* (informal).

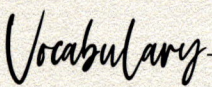 

# Vocabulary

|  |  |
|---|---|
| Scala mobile | Escalator |
| Ascensore | Lift |
| Cintura di sicurezza | Seat belt |
| Biglietto aereo | Plane ticket |

|  |  |
|---|---|
| Avanti | Come in |
| Il Visto? | The Visa? |
| Si' accomodi, prego. | Make yourself comfortable Come in. |
| Passaporto prego… | Passport, please… |
| Eccolo! | Here it is! |

# Renewal of residence permit

1. As soon as you arrive in the Country you will need to ensure that you have an entry Visa (Visto di ingresso) linked to your valid Passport (Passaporto).

2. If you want to study in Italy then simply having an entry Visa is not enough- you will need to have a Residence Permit (Permesso di Soggiorno) in the Country.

   : You will need to apply for this within **8 days of your arrival**
   : You can do this at the Police Headquarters (Questura) of the city where you will be residing
   : After this initial step, you will be able to go online to complete the remainder of the application.

If you plan to stay in Italy beyond the expiry date of your Residence Permit, it will be necessary to apply for an extension of its validity. The procedure for doing so is outlined below:

   : If you have a two-year permit, you will need to apply to renew it ninety days before its expiry date. If you have a one-year permit, the application for renewal will be due sixty days before expiry. The deadline for renewal applications is 30 days for the other categories of Residence Permit.

   : The renewal can be done at the Police Headquarters (Questura) of your city of residence in Italy.

# Permesso di soggiorno

: You will need to purchase a kit for renewal from a post office. The total cost should be around €80, including the stamps and printing charges.

: You will also need 4 passport-sized photos (with a white background).

: You can complete the process independently by sending the papers to the post office, but most people find it helpful to seek the assistance of an experienced local orientation service

: If you miss these deadlines you will have to go to the Questura with a lawyer (who is experienced in migration law). You will have to explain why you failed to renew the permit within the required time period, and you must attempt to apply for late renewal.

---

The validity period of the Permesso di Soggiorno may not, in any situation, exceed:

: Three months, for business or tourism.

: One year, for a course of tudy or job training.
Student permits for courses of more than one year may be renewed annually.

: Two years, for independent work, subordinate permanent work, or for family reunification.

# Vocabulary

|  |  |
|---|---|
| Questura | Police department |
| Carabinieri | Carabineer |
| Polizia | Police |
| Permesso di soggiorno | Permit to stay |
| Visto d'ingresso | Entry visa |
| Prefettura UTG | Prefecture office |
| Sportello unico per l'immigrazione | Unified Desk for immigration |

|  |  |
|---|---|
| Devo rinnovare il mio permesso di soggiorno | I have to renew my residential permit |
| Documenti prego... | Documents please... |
| Sarà pronto entro una settimana! | It will be ready in one week's time! |

# Documents you must always carry in Italy

Make sure that you always carry the following documents with you when outside, as the Police may request to see them. Keep copies in a safe place at home, and do not let anyone take them away without your permission.

1: a. **Your Residence Permit:** Permesso di Soggiorno, or

   b. **The European Union Long-term Residence Permit:** Permesso di Soggiorno UE per Soggiornanti di Lungo Periodo (ex Carta di Soggiorno) .

2. **Your Identity Card** (Carta di'Identità).

   Any person over 15 years of age residing in Italy is eligible for this ID Proof.

   You can request it through the website of the Municipality Office (Comune), or personally apply at the General Registry Office of the Municipality Office (Ufficio Anagrafe Civile Comunale).

   You will receive the card once the local Municipal Police (Polizia Municipale) have verified that you actually reside at the Italian address you provided.

   **Remember that this card is NOT an acceptable ID Proof when you travel to other European countries.**

3. **Your Health Insurance Card** with your Social Security Number (Tessera Sanitaria and Codice Fiscale)

**Remember that, if you leave Italy, you will need to take your passport and your Permit to Stay.**

At the General Registry Office of the Municipality Office you may also place a request for a Residence Certificate
(Certificato di Residenza) or a certificate of Family Status
(Stato di Famiglia).

Cefalú, Italia

# Practicalities of living in Italy

# Finding an accommodation

There are plenty of options for short or long term rental in Italian towns and cities.

Depending on budget, location, and family requirements, you might choose to rent a house (casa), flat (appartamento), or a room (camera).

If your budget is very tight, it is also possible to arrange to take a bed in a shared room (posto letto).

Whichever option you choose, you must ensure that the following conditions are met:

1. You must sign a Contract of Lodgement (Contratto di Affitto) with the landlord.

2. Read this contract carefully before signing.

3. This contract must be registered at the local registration office (Ufficio Registro). You should pay half of the charges for this, your landlord should pay the other half.

4. The landlord will require copies of your photograph and Residence Permit.

5. He/She will use these to fill out a Cessione di Fabbricato form and register you at the police station.

6. It is typical a common procedure to pay three month's rent in advance, some of which might act as the deposit (caparra, deposito)

7. Ensure that you retain receipts for all the payments you make, and take photographs which detail the condition of the room or house before you move in.

> Inside the universities you will find student information bulletin boards, where there will be accommodation offers.
>
> To search for short term apartment rentals, you can check on AirBnb, which offers a wide range of possibilities in the big Italian cities.

# Vocabulary

|  |  |
|---|---|
| Affitto | Rent |
| Bagno | Bathroom |
| Camera | Bedroom |
| Soggiorno | Living room |
| Balcone | Balcony |
| Cucina | Kitchen |
| Letto | Bed |
| Tavolo | Table |
| Sedia | Chair |
| Divano | Sofa |
| Armadio | Wardrobe |
| Credenza | Sideboard |

# Vocabulary

| Bolletta della luce | Electricity bill |
|---|---|
| Bolletta dell'acqua | Water bill |
| Bolletta del gas | Gas bill |

| Monolocale | Studio apartment |
|---|---|
| Bilocale | 1 Bedroom apartment |
| Trilocale | 2 Bedroom apartment |

| Spese condominiali incluse | Condominium fee included |
|---|---|
| Spese escluse | Other expenditures excluded |
| Riscaldamento centralizzato | Central heating |
| Riscaldamento autonomo | Autonomous heating |

# Conversation

| | |
|---|---|
| A che piano è l'appartamento? | On which floor is the apartment? |
| Quanto è l'affitto? | How much is the rent? |
| Quante stanze ha la casa? | How many rooms does the house have? |
| Buongiorno, sto cercando un appartamento | Good Morning, I am looking for an apartment |
| Quanti bagni ci sono? | How many bathrooms are there? |
| 500 euro al mese per la camera doppia | 500 euro per month for the double room |
| Vorrei prendere in affitto una stanza singola… | I would like to rent a single room… |

Jodhpur City
Rajasthan, India

# Healthcare

The Servizio Sanatario Nazionale (SSN) is the National Health System of Italy. Every citizen of the Country and foreign national living in the country must register with the SSN. This can be done at your Local Sanitary Unit

Azienda Sanataria Locale : ASL

Once you have registered, you are entitled to the same health care treatment as any Italian national (provided you have a valid residence permit). Health services are also guaranteed to your family members living in Italy (but not to parents over the age of 65).

**The ASL:**

Your local ASL should be your first point of contact to arrange for most medical requirements in Italy. At the ASL you can select and register with your family doctor and paediatrician, and arrange for home visits from the doctor or from specialists.

You can also procure prescriptions for medication, any vaccinations you may require and any medical certificates needed. You may request tests or examinations from a doctor at the ASL.

If you need to access additional services, such as family planning, maternity support, abortions, vaccinations for children, or pharmaceutical support, you may ask for guidance at the ASL.

# Vocabulary

|  |  |
|---|---|
| Medico di famiglia | Family doctor |
| Pediatra | Paediatrician |
| Certificati medici | Medical certificates |
| Ricette | Prescriptions |
| Richieste | Requests |
| Analisi | Tests |
| Esami medici | Medical examinations |
| Visite specialistiche | Specialist visits |
| Visita domiciliare | Home visit |
| Vaccinazioni obbligatorie | Mandatory vaccinations |
| Consultorio familiare | Family planning centre |
| Cure per la maternità | Maternity care |
| Vaccinazioni per i bambini | Children's vaccinations |
| Interruzione volontaria della gravidanza | Voluntary termination of pregnancy |
| Assistenza farmaceutica | Pharmaceutical assistance |

# Vocabulary

|  |  |
|---|---|
| Farmacia | Chemist shop |
| Ospedale | Hospital |
| Termometro | Thermometer |
| Cerotti | Plasters |
| Farmaci | Drugs |

Matera - la città sotterranea
UNESCO World Heritage Site, Italia

# Healthcare

### The Tessera Sanitaria:

You will need to acquire a Tessera Sanitaria card before you can receive medical treatment from the SSN in Italy. It is a health insurance card which can be used throughout the country and the rest of the European Union.

The card is valid for as long as your Permit to Stay is valid, and you must contact the ASL in order to renew it. You will need to present your renewed Permit to Stay, or documentation to prove that you have applied for its renewal.

If you are staying in Italy only on a temporary basis, then you may obtain an STP code, which entitles you to outpatient and inpatient medical care in the case of a disease or accident. You can get your code from any ASL, University Hospital, or IRCCS (Scientific Institute for Admission and Treatment).

It is not required to show an ID Proof before receiving your STP code, and any data which is recorded via the code cannot be released except under certain legal or criminal circumstances. The code is valid for a period of six months, after which it can be renewed.

# Healthcare

## In Case of Emergency

If you encounter an emergency which requires urgent treatment, call 118 to summon an ambulance. If possible, you could also make your own way to the First Aid (Pronto Soccorso) unit of a hospital.

If you feel that you don't need to go to hospital, but need emergency assistance outside of normal working hours, then you may contact the Guardia Medica.

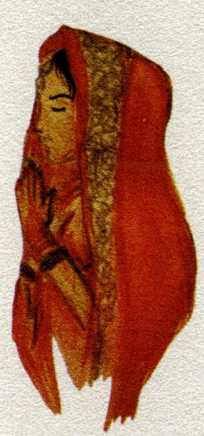

Duomo di Milano
Milano, Italia

# Conversation

|  |  |
|---|---|
| Buongiorno dottore, oggi non mi sento bene | Good morning Doctor, today I am not feeling good |
| Cosa si sente? | How do you feel? |
| Mi fa male la testa | I have a headache |
| Credo di avere la febbre | I believe I have a fever |
| Mangi in bianco per un paio di giorni | Don't eat oily food for a couple of days |
| Si riposi per una settimana | Take rest for a week |

# Transportation

You will find that the public transportation system in most Italian towns and cities is very good.

**Local Travel:**
Take a bus, metro and local trains or trams to travel within the town/city. Visit a tabacchi shop, ticket machine, or station to purchase your ticket before you board. It is also possible to purchase tickets online. If you want to save money on local transport then purchase a transportation pass from the Local Transportation Office. You may be eligible for a discount on the daily, weekly, or monthly passes, so show a copy of your ISEE to show the staff.

Remember! You must validate your ticket once on board.

**Travelling Further Afield:**
If you need to travel longer distances then you can take the train (treno) or, for a cheaper ticket, the long distance bus.

Visit the provider websites to check timetables, make reservations, and buy tickets.

Some Providers:
- : Trenitalia (trains)
- : Italo (trains)
- : GoEuro (buses)
- : Flixbus (buses)
- : Ibus (buses)

# Transportation

Remember! Italy is very well connected, and you can easily pick the cheapest travel option available at the moment of your trip. Many cities in Italy are connected by low cost flights, and it is often cheaper than taking the train.

Also remember that there are diverse rail options, each offering different speeds and prices. You can choose an high speed train or a regional train.

**High speed train – Treni ad alta velocità:**
Freccia Rossa
Freccia Argento
Freccia Bianca

Leh, Ladakh
Jammu and Kashmir, India

# Vocabulary

|  |  |
|---|---|
| Treno | Train |
| Auto | Car |
| Aereo | Plane |
| Pulman | Bus |
| Autobus | Bus |
| Prima classe | First class |
| Seconda classe | Second class |
| Biglietto solo andata | One way ticket |
| Biglietto andata e ritorno | Round trip |
| Treni interregionali | Inter-regional Train |
| Treni locali | Local Train |

|  |  |
|---|---|
| Autostrada | Espressway |
| A destra | To the right |
| A sinistra | To the left |
| Dritto | Straight ahead |

# Conversation

| | |
|---|---|
| Un biglietto, per favore | A ticket, please |
| Un biglietto per Roma, per favore | A ticket to Rome please |
| A che ora parte il treno per Milano? | At what time does the train for Milan leave? |
| Da che binario? | From which platform? |
| Aspetti! | Wait! |
| Dove è la stazione? | Where is the station? |

# Transportation

### Driving

If you want to drive in Italy it is compulsory to hold a valid license.

If you have an Indian driving license, you will need to obtain an international driving permit as well as an official Italian translation of your driving license.

After you have held an Italian residence permit for 12 months you will have to convert your Indian license into an Italian license (conversione della patente di guida). This is cheaper than applying for a new Italian license, and you can do this at the Driver and Vehicle Licensing Agency (Motorizzazione Civile).

If you decide to obtain an Italian driving license then you will need to pass a theoretical examination and a written test. Many people choose to take classes at a private school (scuola guida) in order to prepare. Once you are ready, you can apply to take the tests (esami della patente) at the local Motorizzazione Civile. Remember to take your Residence Permit with you.

### Bicycling

Many people ride bicycles in Italy. If you choose to do so you must be very careful- always wear a helmet, use lights, and stay on quiet roads with special cycle lanes.

# Conversation

|  |  |
|---|---|
| Dove va questa strada? | Where does this road go? |
| Quale è la strada per Venezia? | Which is the road for Venice? |
| Giri a destra al prossimo semaforo | Turn right at the next traffic light |
| Lei è in questo punto su questa carta | You are at this point on this map |
| È lontano? | Is it far? |
| Circa 50 chilometri | Around 50 kilometres |
| Non lo so, mi spiace | I don't know, I am sorry |
| ...attraversi... | ...cross... |

Manarola in Cinque Terre
Liguria, Italia

# Travel and Lodging

You are about to land in a place where beauty is preserved and spread:

Think of that little boot floating in the Mediterranean,
The green of the basil,
The red of the tomato,

And the white snow of the Alps:
The mountain chain which decorates the head of that little peninsula like a crown.

Oh, the Neapolitan pizza;
Oh, the art, the paintings, the sculptures of Florence;
Oh, music- opera in June in Verona...
Oh, Milanese fashion;
Oh, Puglian beaches
And the sea of Sicily and Sardinia;
Extra virgin olive oil, spaghetti...;
Oh, Italian cinema!

Oh, the language,
with that romantic accent which enchants the world;

Oh, the culture of the '*Bel Paese*' and of the '*Dolce vita*'...

Give leisure to your imagination, because here you will find something to delight every sense..

# Vocabulary

| | |
|---|---|
| Data di arrivo | Arrival date |
| Data di partenza | Departure date |
| Bagagli | Baggage |
| Conto | Bill |
| Colazione | Breakfast |
| Chiave | Key |
| Ingresso | Lobby |
| Disponibilità | Availability |
| Pensione completa | Full board |
| Mezza pensione | Half board |
| Servizio in camera | Room service |

# Conversation

| | |
|---|---|
| Vorrei una stanza per una notte | I'd like a room for the night |
| Per non fumatori | I'd like a non-smoking room |
| Non c'è l'acqua calda | There is no hot water |
| Ho una prenotazione | I have a reservation |
| A quale nome? | In which name? |
| Può chiamarmi un taxi per l'aeroporto? | Can you call me a taxi for the airport? |
| Sì, arriverà tra 10 minuti | Yes, it will arrive in 10 minutes |
| A che ora è il check-out domani? | At what time is the check out tomorrow? |

# Conversation

| | |
|---|---|
| Buongiorno vorrei chiedere delle informazioni | Good morning, I would like to have some information |
| Che tipo di eventi ci saranno in città? | What kind of events will be there in town? |
| Mi piace molto l'arte, può consigliarmi qualche museo? | I really like art, can you suggest some museums for me? |
| Che tipo di spettacoli saranno organizzati per capodanno? | What kind of show will be organized during the new year's eve? |
| Potete propormi qualche itinerario specifico? | Can you offer me some specific itinerary? |
| Salve, sa come posso raggiungere l'università? | Hello, do you know how to reach the university? |
| La biblioteca dove si trova? | Do you know where the library is? |

# Conversation

| | |
|---|---|
| A che ora inizia la conferenza in Aula Magna? | At what time does the conference in the great hall start? |
| Quale autobus devo prendere per raggiungere la facoltà? | Which bus do I have to take to go to the university? |
| E' molto lontana Piazza Garibaldi da qui? | Is it very far to get to Garibaldi's square from here? |
| Qual è la fermata della metro più vicina? | Which is the closest metro stop from here? |

Confluence of River Indus and Zanskar
Ladakh, India

# Taking language courses

In Italy, it is a necessary requirement for foreign nationals to take lessons in the Italian language, culture, and civilisation. If you partake in these lessons you will gain credits which will exempt you from future verification tests (as per the Integration Agreement- Accordo Di Integrazione).

Various organisations run free classes. Visit the Centri Territoriali Permanenti per l'Educazione degli Adulti (CTPs) to gather information about the timings and locations of such classes.

You may also want to attendan evening course (corsi serali) to further your education, or even to work towards a qualification or certification. The Ministry of Education offers a number of such courses- ranging from lower secondary school diplomas (licenza media inferiore) to high school diplomas, as well as vocational training programmes and classes in Italian law, culture, and language.

**Staying in Italy after completing your studies:**

Once you have finished your course, your Residence Permit will remain valid until its expiry date. However, once the renewal is due, if you want to remain in Italy you will have to apply at the Prefettura UTG for a 6 month permit extension. During this time it will be necessary for you to secure employment if you want to remain in the Country for a longer period of time.

# Employment in Italy

If you are over 16 years of age and have an identity document, a valid Residence Permit, and your Codice Fiscale, you can register for free with the local State Job Centre (Centro per l'Impiego, or CPI) in order to find a job.

International students are allowed to work for a maximum of 20 hours per week, and are entitled to be paid at least the minimum wage.
You must have a work contract which clearly sets your pay and working hours. If you do not have this it will be impossible to renew your Residence Permit because your employment will be considered unofficial.

In fact it is illegal to work without a proper contract, or to be paid in cash with no receipt. It is called irregular work or black work (lavoro irregolare or lavoro in nero), and it means that your employer will not be paying taxes or insurance on your behalf.

**What to do in case of an employment dispute:**

If you find yourself in conflict with your employer, or you are unsure about the legality of your work or employment status, get in touch with a trade union or with a lawyer. You may also seek help at the offices of the local sindacati, where you can find support in filing a case against your employer. They may help you to reclaim unpaid wages or organise court proceedings.

Auli
Uttarakhand, India

# Banking and Finance

Foreigners in Italy, resident or non-resident, are entitled to open an Italian bank account (conto bancario).

In order to do so, you should visit a branch of the bank you want to open an account with. You may also seek the help of an external agency which specialises in helping immigrants to access banking services in Italy (they will usually demand a fee for such services).

You will need to show the following documents in order to open your account:

1. An identity document (Identity card/Passport/Visa)
2. Your tax code (codice fiscale);
3. Your residence permit (or any other official document that is a proof of residence);
4. Proof of employment/self-employment status (contract, income tax return etc.).

Once the bank has approved your request to open an account, you will be able to set up your online and mobile banking, make deposits, and withdraw funds.

Make sure that you pay attention to the account's rules and restrictions regarding debit/credit cards, ATM withdrawals, fees, foreign transfers, fixed costs, interest payments etc.

# Vocabulary

| | |
|---|---|
| Conto corrente | Bank account |
| Bancomat | ATM card |
| Carta di credito | Credit card |
| Bonifico | Transfer |
| Soldi | Money |

| | |
|---|---|
| Dove firmo? | Where do I sign? |
| Dove è lo sportello? | Where is the cashier's window? |
| Quale è il cambio oggi? | What is the currency exchange rate today? |

Many Indian students don't have a surname on their passport! This is a big problem when applying for a bank account in Italy.

Your tax code (Codice Fiscale) will begin with XXX, which is unacceptable for banks.

Please keep in mind that we won't be able to help you with this problem!

Galleria Vittorio Emanuele II
Milano, Italia

# Shopping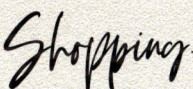

Italy is famous all over the world for its rich textile, leather design and excellence in craftsmanship. Milan, one of the fashion capitals of the world, exemplifies this gloriously.

Italy is well-known for its fashion goods, in both quality and superior craftsmanship and skills. Italy has exceptional quality of leather products which are created with utmost excellence and attention to detail. Italian fashion has a long tradition, and is regarded as one most important influences in the world of fashion.

Major Italian fashion labels, such as Gucci, Armani, Prada, Versace, Valentino, Dolce & Gabbana, Missoni, Fendi, Moschino, Max Mara, Trussardi, and Ferragamo, to name a few, are regarded as among the finest fashion houses in the world.

Italy is also home to some of the best meat, cheese and wines of the world. There are plenty of options for food and drinks.

> **Remember that in Italy the size of the clothes and the size of the shoes are different!**
>
> Shoes: 37, 38, 39…..
> Pants: 38,40,42…..
> T-shirt: xs, s, m, l……
> Underwear: 1st, 2nd, 3rd….

# Vocabulary

|  |  |
|---|---|
| Negozio di alimentari | Grocery shop |
| Supermercato | Supermarket |
| Macelleria | Butcher shop |
| Fruttivendolo | Fruit and vegetable shop |
| Negozio di abbigliamento | Clothes shop |
| Panetteria | Bakery |
| Gelateria | Ice-cream shop |
| Pasticceria | Pastry shop |

# Vocabulary

| Le scarpe | Shoes |
|---|---|
| La borsa | Bag |
| Una maglietta | T-shirt |
| I pantaoni | Pants |
| Una gonna | Skirt |
| I calzini | Socks |
| Una camicia | Shirt |
| Un maglione | Sweater |
| Una giacca | Jacket |

Rein in Taufers
Sud Tirolo, Italia

# Conversation

| | |
|---|---|
| Quanto costa? | How much does it cost? |
| C'è lo sconto? | Is there any discount? |
| Posso pagare con la carta? | Can I pay with a credit card? |
| Mi può aiutare, per favore? | Can you help me please? |
| Come posso aiutarla? | How can I help you? |
| Sto solo dando uno sguardo | I am just looking |
| Ha un altro colore? | Do you have another color? |

# Emergency details

| Name of organization | Local Offices |
|---|---|
| **Ambulanza**<br>Ambulance, First Aid | 112 |
| **Vigili del fuoco**<br>Fire brigade | 112 |
| **Forze dell'ordine**<br>Police<br>Carabineer | 112 |
| **National Anti Dicrimination Office**<br>Assistance for victims<br>of racial discrimination | 800901010<br>www.unar.it |

You can call 112 from mobile even if there is no network, if the credit is exhausted or if the smartphone is blocked by the PIN.

Obviously, the number remains free from both landline and mobile.

# Conversation

| | |
|---|---|
| Mi lasci stare! | Leave me alone! |
| Chiamo la polizia! | I'll call the police! |
| Non mi tocchi! | Don't touch me! |
| Polizia! | Police! |
| Al ladro! | Thief! |
| È un emergenza! | It's an emergency! |

# Conversation

|  |  |
|---|---|
| Mi sono perso | I am lost |
| Ho perso il portafogli | i have lost my wallet |
| Aiuto! | Help! |
| Ho bisogno del suo aiuto | I need your help! |
| Mi hanno rubato la borsa | Someone stole my bag |
| Vuole sporgere denuncia? | Do you want to file a complaint? |

# Contacts in Delhi

**Embassy of Italy**
www.ambnewdelhi.esteri.it
ambasciata.newdelhi@esteri.it
newdelhi.study@esteri.it


**Italian Embassy Cultural Centre**
https://iicnewdelhi.esteri.it/iic_newdelhi/it/
iicnewdelhi@esteri.it


**Uni-Italia**
http://www.uni-italia.net/india
newdelhi@uni-italia.it

Assisi
Umbria, Italia

# Greetings

| Buongiorno | Good morning |
|---|---|
| Buona giornata | Have a good day |
| Buon pomeriggio | Good afternoon |
| Buona sera | Good evening |
| Buona serata | Have a good evening |
| Buona notte | Good night |
| Buona notte, Laura | Good night, Laura |

| Ciao | Hi |
|---|---|
| Salve | Hello (polite way) |
| Arrivederci Pranjay | Good bye Pranjay (polite way) |
| ArrivederLa dottore | Good bye Doctor (very polite way) |
| A presto Yuvraj! | See you soon Yuvraj! |
| Alla prossima volta, Paola! | See you next time Paola! |

# Polite expressions

|  |  |
|---|---|
| Per favore | Please |
| Per piacere | Please |
| Grazie | Thanks |
| Grazie molto! | Thank you very much! |
| Molte grazie | Many thanks |
| Grazie tante | Thanks a lot |
| Grazie mille | A thousand thanks |
| Prego | You're welcome |
| Di niente! | You're welcome! |
| Permesso? | May I (enter)? |
| Grazie, Maryam | Thank you, Maryam |

|  |  |
|---|---|
| Si | Yes |
| Certo | Of course |
| D'accordo | I agree |
| Penso di si | I think so |

# Introduction

| | |
|---|---|
| Come ti chiami? | What is your name? |
| Mi chiamo Paola! | My name is Paola! |
| E tu? | And you? |
| Sono Yash | I'm Yash |
| Piacere | Nice to meet you |

# Introduction

**Polite Way**

| | |
|---|---|
| Come si chiama? | What is your name? |
| Mi chiamo Paola! | My name is Paola! |
| E Lei? | And you? |
| Mi chiamo Yash | My name is Yash |
| Molto liet<u>o</u><br>Molto liet<u>a</u> | Glad to meet you<br><u>o</u> : if you are a man<br><u>a</u> : if you are a woman |

# Introduction

| Polite Way | |
|---|---|
| Lei è il signor…? | Are you Sir…? |
| Singh. Yuvraj Singh. | Singh. Yuvraj Singh. |
| Singh? Anch'io; Dipesh Singh. | Singh? Me too; Dipesh Singh. |
| Piacere di conoscerLa | Nice to meet you |
| Piacere mio | The pleasure is mine |

Lago di Como
Lombardia, Italia

# Conversation

| | |
|---|---|
| Ciao, di dove sei? | Hello, where are you from? |
| Sono Indiana, di Dharamsala. | I am Indian (woman), from Dharamsala. |
| Anche io sono indiano, di Amritsar. | Me too. I am Indian (man), from Amritsar. |

### Polite Way

| | |
|---|---|
| Lei è indiano? (Male) Lei è Indiana? (Female) | Are you Indian? |
| Si, sono di Mumbai | Yes, I am from Mumbai |
| Di dov'è lei? | Where are you from? |
| Sono di Delhi. | I am from Delhi. |

# Conversation

| | |
|---|---|
| Da dove vieni, Vasit? | Where are you from Vasit? |
| Vengo dal nord dell'India, da Nuova Delhi | I come from north India, from New Delhi |
| Quanti anni hai? | How old are you? |
| Ho 21 anni | I'm 21 |

**Polite Way**

| | |
|---|---|
| Quanti anni ha? | How old are you? |
| Ho 21 anni | I'm 21 |

# Numbers and counting

- 1 : Uno
- 2 : Due
- 3 : Tre
- 4 : Quattro
- 5 : Cinque
- 6 : Sei
- 7 : Sette
- 8 : Otto
- 9 : Nove
- 10 : Dieci

- 11 : Undici
- 12 : Dodici
- 13 : Tredici
- 14 : Quattordici
- 15 : Quindici
- 16 : Sedici
- 17 : Diciassette
- 18 : Diciotto
- 19 : Diciannove
- 20 : Venti

# Numbers and counting

- 21 : Ventuno
- 22 : Ventidue
- 23 : Ventitre

... and so on

- 30 : Trenta
- 40 : Quaranta
- 50 : Cinquanta
- 60 : Sessanta
- 70 : Settanta
- 80 : Ottanta
- 90 : Novanta
- 100 : Cento

# Days: I giorni

| | |
|---|---|
| Lunedì | Monday |
| Martedì | Tuesday |
| Mercoledì | Wednesday |
| Giovedì | Thursday |
| Venerdì | Friday |
| Sabato | Saturday |
| Domenica | Sunday |

| | |
|---|---|
| Ieri | Yesterday |
| Oggi | Today |
| Domani | Tomorrow |

| | |
|---|---|
| Mattina | Morning |
| Pomeriggio | Afternoon |
| Sera | Evening |
| Notte | Night |

# Months: I mesi

| | |
|---|---|
| Prima | Before |
| Ora | Now |
| Dopo | Later |

| | |
|---|---|
| Gennaio | January |
| Febbraio | February |
| Marzo | March |
| Aprile | April |
| Maggio | May |
| Giugno | June |
| Luglio | July |
| Agosto | August |
| Settembre | September |
| Ottobre | October |
| Novembre | November |
| Dicembre | December |

Pasta al pomodoro
Italia

# At restaurants

A traditional Italian meal is, as a rule, divided into different courses.

The meal begins with an appetizer - a small portion intended to stimulate the appetite.

Next comes the first course (usually pasta, rice, or soup), and then the second course (meat or fish) accompanied by a side dish of your choice (salad, grilled vegetables, fries ..).

Finally comes the sweet course, followed by fruit and coffee.

Nowadays, however, most Italians no longer follow this traditional structure every day, and instead reserve the meal for Sundays and holidays

# Vocabulary

|  |  |
|---|---|
| Pollo | Chicken |
| Maiale | Pork |
| Agnello | Lamb |
| Coniglio | Rabbit |
| Vitello | Veal |
| Bistecca | Steak |
| Manzo | Beef |
| Pesce | Fish |
| Carne | Meat |
| Verdure | Vegetables |
| Contorno | Side dish |
| Dolce | Dessert |
| Frutta | Fruits |

Pizza con le olive nere
Italia

# Vocabulary

|  |  |
|---|---|
| Vino rosso | Red wine |
| Vino bianco | White wine |
| Vino frizzante | Sparkling wine |
| Vino fermo | Still wine |

|  |  |
|---|---|
| Vorrei…. | I would like… |
| Un pò (di)… | Some of … |
| Questo… | this… |
| Quello… | that… |

# Conversation

| | |
|---|---|
| Cosa desidera? | What would you like? |
| Vorrei un caffe, per favore | I would like a coffee, please |
| Buongiorno, avete un tavolo per due persone? | Good morning, is there a table available for 2 people? |
| Quale piatto consiglia lo chef? | Which dish does the chef suggest? |
| Come primo prendo gli spaghetti alla carbonara e come secondo una bistecca ai ferri | As first course I would like spaghetti alla carbonara, as second course one grilled steak |
| Sono vegetariano | I am vegetarian |
| Mi porta il conto, per favore? | Can I have the bill, please? |

# Useful Questions

| Per favore, Maria... | Please, Maria... |

| C'è qualcuno che parla inglese? | Does anyone speak English? |

| Permesso? | May I? |

| Parla inglese? | Do you speak English? |

| Può parlare più lentamente? | Can you speak more slowly? |

| Più lentamente, per favore! | Slowly, please! |

Isola di San Pietro
Sardegna, Italia

# Useful Questions

|  |  |
|---|---|
| Capisce? | Do you understand? |
| Non capisco | I don't understand |
| Capisco | I understand |
| Parlo poco l'italiano | I speak a little Italian |
| Cosa vuol dire 'telefonino'? | What does 'telefonino' mean? |
| Mi dispiace! | I'm sorry! |
| Mi scusi! | Excuse me! |

# Useful Questions

| | |
|---|---|
| Come si dice in italiano '*book*'? | How do you say '*book*' in Italian? |
| Si dice '*libro*' | It's '*libro*' |
| Come si scrive '*famiglia*'? | How do you spell '*famiglia*'? |
| Può scriverlo, per favore? | Could you please write it down? |
| Può ripetere, per favore? | Can you repeat it please? |